Fossil Fuels

by Jim Ollhoff

 PRINTED ON RECYCLED PAPER

Editor: John Hamilton
Graphic Design: John Hamilton
Cover Photos: Jupiter Images, iStockphoto
Interior Photo: Getty Images, page 6, 7,14, 15, 18, 20, 22, 23, 25, 26, 27; Jupiterimages, page 17, 19, 20; iStockphoto, page 1, 4, 10, 12, 13, 16; Photo Researchers, page 5, 8, 9, 11.

Library of Congress Cataloging-in-Publication Data

Ollhoff, Jim, 1959-
 Fossil fuels / Jim Ollhoff.
   p. cm. -- (Future energy)
 Includes index.
 ISBN 978-1-60453-935-6
 1. Fossil fuels--Juvenile literature. I. Title.
 TP318.3.O45 2010
 333.8'2--dc22
                    2009029857

Contents

How Fossil Fuels Form

Coal, oil, and natural gas are called fossil fuels. Power plants use these fuels to make electricity. Fossil fuels come from deep underground. Millions of years ago, when prehistoric plants and animals died, their organic matter formed huge deposits. Through the centuries, this organic matter got buried under rock, dirt, and sand. As time went on, the organic matter changed because of pressure, heat, and bacteria. Depending on the conditions and the kind of organic matter, it became oil, coal, or natural gas.

Below: Coal from a mine in Wales, United Kingdom, ready for burning in a power plant.

Oil was formed first in most areas. In deeper and hotter areas, natural gas formed. Coal was formed from the remains of swampy vegetation covered by water. Some people like to say that fossil fuels come from dead dinosaurs, but that's not really true. Fossil fuels come from all kinds of ancient plants and animals—much deposited long before dinosaurs ever existed. So, fossil fuels don't come from fossils. But fossils show plants and animals whose organic matter, in some cases, became coal, oil, and natural gas.

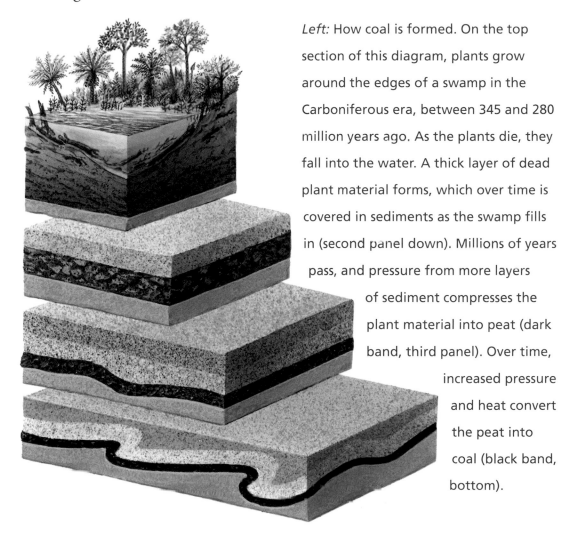

Left: How coal is formed. On the top section of this diagram, plants grow around the edges of a swamp in the Carboniferous era, between 345 and 280 million years ago. As the plants die, they fall into the water. A thick layer of dead plant material forms, which over time is covered in sediments as the swamp fills in (second panel down). Millions of years pass, and pressure from more layers of sediment compresses the plant material into peat (dark band, third panel). Over time, increased pressure and heat convert the peat into coal (black band, bottom).

How Coal is Mined and Burned

There are huge deposits of coal in the United States. There is an eastern region of coal, in states such as West Virginia and Pennsylvania. In the middle region of the country, states such as Illinois and Texas have a lot of coal. In the west, there is a very productive coal-mining region that includes Wyoming and Montana. Almost 40 states have coalfields, but right now coal is only mined in about 25 states.

Below: An open-pit coal mine in Wyoming.

Coal is the remains of ancient plants and animals that accumulated in swamps and peat bogs. The remains were covered with water, then dirt and sand. Heat, pressure, and bacteria pushed the organic material, called carbon, together. Over millions of years the process created the black, rock-like material that burns.

There are four ranks of coal, depending on how much carbon it contains. The more carbon in the coal, the more energy it can produce. Anthracite is the highest-carbon, highest-energy coal. Supplies of anthracite have been nearly used up in the United States, so it is fairly rare. This is followed by bituminous, the most common kind of coal in the United States. Subbituminous coal is the third kind of coal. It is found mostly in western states. Finally, lignite is the type of coal with the lowest efficiency. It is the youngest coal, not subjected to the heat and pressure that made the other kinds of coal. Because lignite is a lower grade of coal, power plants have to burn two or three times as much lignite as anthracite to get the same amount of energy.

Right: Anthracite coal is prized for its high carbon content, which gives it high energy when it burns.

Coal is mined in one of two ways: strip mining or underground mining. In strip mining, sometimes called area mining, the coal is close to the surface. Topsoil and rock are removed and bulldozers scrape up the coal. Then, it is transported to power plants.

Underground mining gets coal that is deeper in the ground. Miners find the coal seam and cut it out of the ground. This process forms tunnels and small underground caverns.

Right: Cutaway artwork of a coal mine showing the seams of coal (black) and the tunnels bored into them. Coal is carved from the seams and is lifted to the surface by a conveyor belt, which then deposits it in piles (upper right).

Coal is usually shipped by train or barge to power plants. The coal is refined by washing with water and chemicals to remove the dirt and some impurities. The coal is crushed into a powder, and then burned. The burning of the coal heats water in pipes. This water turns to steam, which makes turbines spin. Generators convert the motion of the turbines into electricity.

Below: The inside of a coal-burning power station, showing the very large steam turbines and generators.

Coal: Good and Bad

Facing page:
Coal-fired power
plants spew tons of
pollutants into the
air each year.
Below: Coal is
relatively abundant
and cheap.

More than 50 percent of the electricity in the United States comes from coal. While it takes millions of years for nature to make coal, power plants are burning it quickly. To power an average home in North America for 60 days takes one ton (907 kg) of coal. Still, even though our world is burning coal much faster than it can be made, coal is still plentiful. At current rates of consumption, there is enough coal to last more than 150 years. It is also relatively cheap to burn.

The biggest problem with coal is that it is a very dirty fossil fuel. In one year, an average coal plant will put a toxic variety of pollutants into the air, including 114 pounds (52 kg) of lead, 225 (102 kg) pounds of arsenic, and 170 pounds (77 kg) of mercury. A typical coal plant will put 10,000 tons (9,072 metric tons) of sulfur dioxide into the air, the primary cause of acid rain. More than 10,000 tons (9,072 metric tons) of nitrogen oxide is pumped into the air, which causes respiratory problems in many people. An average power plant will put almost four million tons (3.6 million metric tons) of carbon dioxide into the air, which most scientists agree is adding to the greenhouse effect, causing the earth's climate to change.

Above: Giant earth-moving equipment at a strip mine.

Efforts have begun to try to find ways to clean the coal before it is burned. Scientists hope to someday remove the particles and toxins before they get into the air. However, these technological advances will no doubt be very expensive.

Another disadvantage of coal is the problem of getting it out of the ground Strip mining is very damaging to the environment. And underground mining is a dangerous occupation for miners.

Coal has to be transported from the mines to the power plants. This is because coal-mining areas are usually places where water is scarce. A lot of water is needed for the refining of coal. Also, train transportation puts pollutants into the air. Railroad locomotives carrying coal put about one million tons (907,185 metric tons) of nitrogen oxide into the air each year.

Finally, storing coal at power plants is a problem. Usually, coal is stored in huge, uncovered piles. Coal dust blows off the piles, putting pollutants and toxins into the air. Rainwater picks up the pollutants and can contaminate the land.

Below: A coal train on its way to a power plant.

Questions About Oil

Oil comes from 500-million-year-old plants and animals. This organic matter settled and then, over the centuries, was buried by dirt, sand, and rock. Pressure, heat, and bacteria converted the organic material into oil. Since the oil was under pressure, it seeped up toward the surface through porous rock. There, it waited to be discovered. While people have used oil for centuries, the modern period of drilling oil began in the late 1800s and early 1900s.

Oil production companies use massive drills connected by long sections of pipes. The drills cut through the rock and sediment until oil is reached.

After being brought to the surface, the crude oil is transported to refineries, where it is made into useable products, such as gasoline, lubricants, paints, and plastics. About 70 percent of oil is made into gasoline for automobiles and other kinds of transportation.

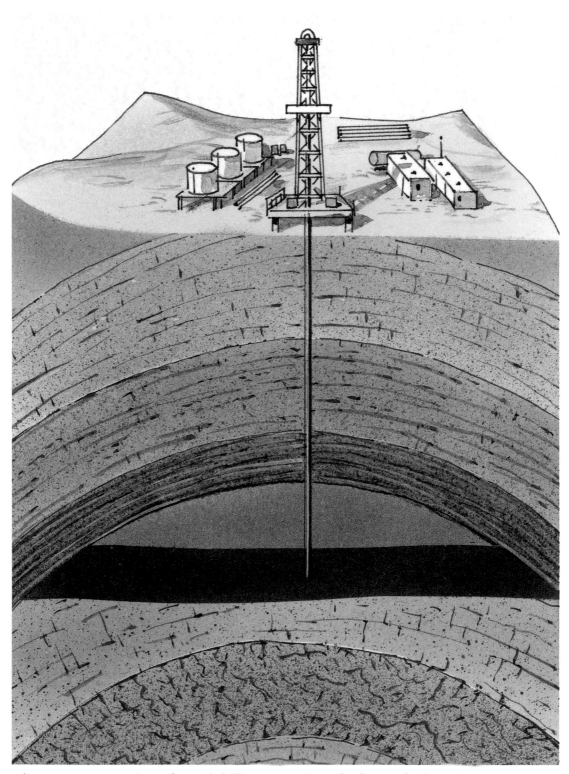

Above: A cutaway view of an oil-drilling operation. The layer of oil is colored black.

The United States gets about half its oil supply from foreign countries. Some of those countries have unstable leadership. Many people believe the United States' oil supply is vulnerable to sudden stoppages or price hikes.

An important questions regarding oil is, "How much is left?" This is a difficult and complex question, with no clear answer. It is hard to say how much oil is left in the ground. When a new oil field is discovered, some of the oil is easy to get out of the ground. Some of the oil is impossible to get out. Some company officials, who want to make their companies sound bigger and richer than they really are, will give the size of an entire oil field, even though they know that most of the oil will never be pulled out.

How much oil is undiscovered? No one knows. Some of the biggest recent discoveries of oil happened in the 1960s. (It is still unclear how much oil is in the recently discovered arctic areas.) Is this because no oil is left to be discovered? Or is it because geologists haven't looked hard enough for new oil fields? No one knows for sure.

Below: An oil refinery at night.

Geologists use the term "Hubbert's peak" to talk about how much oil is left. (Marion King Hubbert was the first geologist to talk about the issue.) Production starts small, and then goes up to a peak. The peak refers to the maximum amount of oil production. After that, oil production begins to decline. Oil becomes harder to get out of the ground and becomes more expensive.

So, when is Hubbert's Peak? No one knows for sure. Some say the peak has already happened. Others say it is 50 to 70 years away, because new technology will make it possible to get more oil out of the ground. Most official estimates say the peak will happen around 2020 to 2030.

Below: Pumpjacks steadily lift crude oil out of the ground.

Oil: Good and Bad

Oil's advantage is that it is currently plentiful and still relatively cheap. All the systems are in place to bring oil to refineries and then get the finished product to gas stations.

One disadvantage of oil is its limited supply. Before oil is exhausted, there are likely to be wild price fluctuations.

Another disadvantage is the danger of oil spills. In the 20 years before 1993, there were almost 200,000 oil spills. One billion gallons (3.8 billion liters) of oil spill or leak into oceans and waterways every year.

Large oil spills can be a disaster to the environment. One of the biggest oil spills was the *Exxon Valdez* spill in the pristine waters of Prince William Sound in Alaska in 1989. It spilled nearly 11 million gallons (41.6 million liters), killing wildlife and washing crude oil up onto coasts.

One of the biggest oil polluters, however, is parked in the garage. The gasoline from automobiles creates huge amounts of pollutants and carbon dioxide.

Below: Vehicles consume huge amounts of oil products and emit pollutants into the atmosphere.

Natural Gas

Natural gas is a fossil fuel formed by ancient plants and animals that were covered by rock and submitted to intense heat and pressure. Natural gas is often found mixed together with oil. It is sometimes called the "prince of hydrocarbons" because it is the cleanest of the fossil fuels. Methane is the main ingredient in natural gas.

In the late 1800s and early 1900s, people wanted oil instead of natural gas. So, thinking that the gas was just waste, they burned it away. No one knows how much gas was lost this way.

Early in the 1900s, people used gas to power streetlights and light buildings. Soon, it became clear that natural gas was valuable and useful. By the 1950s, pipelines were built to carry gas to facilities where it could be stored and used.

Today, most natural gas is used for heating in furnaces, stoves, and water heaters. Some natural gas is used to help make steel, plastics, and chemicals. Some natural gas is also used for electricity.

Left: About one-fifth of the natural gas consumed in the United States is used in residences to cook or heat homes.

Above: A natural gas refinery.

Natural Gas: Good & Bad

Facing page: Drilling and extraction of oil and natural gas continues to put pressure on the environment. *Below:* A tanker filled with liquefied natural gas.

Compared to coal, natural gas is very clean. It produces no solid waste and very little sulfur dioxide. It has become very popular because it is so clean. It is also very cheap to pipe from one location to another.

However, because it is a carbon-based fuel, natural gas releases carbon dioxide, a major greenhouse gas. It also releases nitrogen oxides, which cause acid rain and smog. When natural gas leaks out into the atmosphere, its main ingredient is methane. Methane is a more potent greenhouse gas than carbon dioxide.

While it is cheaper to transport than oil or coal,

there are still environmental impacts to transport gas by ship or truck. Technological advances have decreased the environmental impacts, but it is still not as clean as renewable sources such as wind or solar power.

Geologists are not sure how much natural gas is left in the world. Oil will probably run out before natural gas. Some estimates suggest natural gas will run out by 2075.

Fixes For Fossil Fuels

Fossil fuels are inexpensive. The system is already in place to make use of them. However, they release pollutants that cause damage to the environment and create health problems for people. Can new technological developments fix the problems?

Many people hope that someday there will be clean coal. Engineering advances might provide filters that scrub out pollutants before coal is burned. Right now, the technology to do that doesn't exist, but perhaps advancements will come in the future. However, such advancements will probably be very expensive, which will mean that coal will no longer be such a cheap source of electricity.

Facing page: A power plant at night, generating electricity. Scientists are hard at work today, trying to find ways to use fossil fuels without harming the environment.

When coal is burned, it releases carbon dioxide into the atmosphere. Scientists are working on a way to remove the carbon dioxide before it gets into the air. They hope to somehow capture it and store it in a safe place. This is called carbon sequestration. Scientists have discussed storing the carbon dioxide deep underground or deep in the ocean. So far, no good economical option exists, but perhaps that will change in the future.

Known supplies of natural gas will probably run out within this century. Could new sources of natural gas be found? Scientists are experimenting with giant buildings called digesters. These buildings process dead vegetation. The decay creates methane, the primary ingredient in natural gas. Could giant digesters increase the reserves of natural gas in an economical way? So far, no one knows for sure.

There is a type of rock called oil shale, which contains large amounts of organic matter. Through a refining process, synthetic crude oil can be produced from this shale. Oil shale is sometimes called a non-conventional fossil fuel. Right now, the refining process creates a lot of pollution. But might it extend the reserves of oil? Nobody really knows for sure.

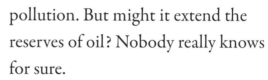

Could engineers create a way to increase the efficiency of fossil fuels? Might scientists find other non-conventional fossil fuels? Could scientists find ways of transporting and storing fossil fuels that are cleaner? Scientists are working on all of these issues. Time will tell whether they are successful or not.

Left: Oil shale igniting. If scientists can invent a new refining process, oil shale might extend our oil reserves.

Above: The egg-shaped digesters at Deer Island in Massachusetts use dead vegetation to create methane fuel, which is then used to make electricity.

The Future of Fossil Fuels

There is no question that fossil fuels will be a significant source of electricity for the foreseeable future. Coal, oil, and natural gas are already in place. For the time being, they are cheap and easily accessible.

However, almost everyone realizes that fossil fuels won't be around forever. A transition to renewable fuels is necessary. The sooner that renewables can become the main source of electricity, the better.

The biggest disaster would be if oil peaked and suddenly became very expensive, and society was caught unprepared. A plan is needed now to transition off of fossil fuels.

The problem can be solved with a clear, intentional movement toward power generated by the sun, wind, water, and other renewables. Conserving electricity will be very important during the transition.

In the meantime, until we transition to renewables, we will continue to need fossil fuels.

Glossary

ACID RAIN

Rain, or other kind of precipitation, that has a high concentration of acid. It is harmful to plants and many buildings. Most acid rain is caused by burning fossil fuels, which releases sulfur, nitrogen, and carbon into the air. These react with water in the atmosphere to make rain more acidic than is found naturally.

BITUMINOUS

A form of coal that is very common in North America.

CARBON DIOXIDE

Normally a gas, carbon dioxide is a chemical compound made up of two oxygen atoms and one carbon atom. Its chemical symbol is CO_2. Carbon dioxide in the earth's atmosphere acts as a greenhouse gas.

CARBON SEQUESTRATION

The process of capturing carbon dioxide before it gets into the atmosphere and storing it in a safe place, such as deep underground.

FOSSIL FUEL

Fuels that are created by the remains of ancient plants and animals that were buried and then subjected to millions of years of heat, pressure, and bacteria. Oil and coal are the most common fossil fuels burned to create electricity. Natural gas is also a fossil fuel. Burning fossil fuels releases carbon dioxide into the atmosphere, contributing to global warming.

Greenhouse Effect

The earth naturally warms because of the greenhouse effect. The surface of the earth absorbs some solar radiation, and reflects some. The reflected rays either pass back into space, or are absorbed and reflected back by gasses in the earth's atmosphere. Carbon dioxide is a major greenhouse gas that is produced by burning fossil fuels. When too much solar radiation is absorbed, the earth warms up, which alters climates around the world.

Greenhouse Gas

Any gas that is good at absorbing and retaining the sun's heat. Carbon dioxide, which is released into the atmosphere by the burning of fossil fuels, is a greenhouse gas.

Hubbert's Peak

A way of describing the production of oil. The peak is the maximum production of oil, after which production falls and oil becomes more scarce and more expensive.

Renewable Energy

Any kind of energy where the source won't get used up. Wind power, waterpower, and solar power are examples of renewable energy.

Strip Mining

A way of mining coal that creates a giant open pit, instead of digging underground in mines.

Index